CELEBRATING ALL FAMILIES

BY ABBY COLICH

BLUE OWL
BOOKS

TIPS FOR CAREGIVERS

Social and emotional learning (SEL) helps children manage emotions, learn how to feel empathy, create and achieve goals, and make good decisions. Strong lessons and support in SEL will help children establish positive habits in communication, cooperation, and decision-making. By incorporating SEL in early reading, children will learn the importance of accepting and celebrating all people in their communities.

BEFORE READING

Talk to the reader about families. Ask what he or she thinks a family is.

Discuss: What is one way your family is like another family you know? What is one way your family is different?

AFTER READING

Talk to the reader about ways he or she can celebrate his or her family's differences with others.

Discuss: What is one way you can celebrate your family? How can you accept another family? Why is it good for members of a community to accept one another?

SEL GOAL

Children may have a loose understanding of acceptance. Talk to readers about the importance of empathy in accepting and celebrating the differences of others. Have they ever felt singled out for having a different family? What did it feel like? If they haven't experienced this, ask them to imagine what it feels like. Make a list of these different feelings. Then ask readers to list the feelings they have when they are included and accepted. Explain that our communities are better when everyone is accepted and included.

TABLE OF CONTENTS

CHAPTER 1
Many Kinds of Families..4

CHAPTER 2
Respect All Families...12

CHAPTER 3
Celebrate All Families...18

GOALS AND TOOLS
Grow with Goals..22
Writing Reflection...22
Glossary...23
To Learn More..23
Index...24

MANY KINDS OF FAMILIES

Who is in your family? Do you have a few family members or many? Families can be large or small. Every family is different. There is no wrong way to be a family.

Families of all different sizes, ages, and kinds are in every **community**. Every family is its own community, too!

People in a family are **related** to one another. Some are related by blood. Some are related by **marriage** or **adoption**. Some families are **blended**. It doesn't matter how a family came to be. All families are part of a community.

FAMILIES CHANGE

Families can change. New children are born, and people pass away. Couples can get married or **divorced**. These events all create new families.

Your **household** can be different from your family. Your household is made up of the people you live with. Janessa lives with a **foster family**. She has other family members who she doesn't live with.

Evie lives with her mom half of the time and her dad half of the time. She is part of two households.

LIKE FAMILY

Have you ever heard the phrase "like family"? Some people may not be related to you, but they feel like family. You love them and spend a lot of time with them. They may even live with you! They are "like family."

Family members are close with each other. They love and care for one another. This doesn't mean there aren't arguments. Whitney argues with her brother. But later they say they are sorry. They still **support** each other.

CHAPTER 2

RESPECT ALL FAMILIES

We respect our family members. We should also respect other families, even if they look different from ours. Lucy lives with her grandparents. Together, they make up a small family. She does not have any siblings.

Juan has many siblings! These families are different, but we treat them the same. One family is not better than another.

We respect other families by showing **empathy**. This means trying to understand how someone feels. Misha is an only child. Mark asks her about it. He tries to imagine what it would feel like to not have siblings. He invites Misha over. They all play together!

When you take time to learn about other families, you may find they are more like yours than you thought. Jay is new at school. You find out his family goes to the pool on the weekends, too! Your family invites his family to meet you there. Fun!

CELEBRATE ALL FAMILIES

Claire's neighbor is a single mom. Claire helps their family. She walks the older kids to school. She babysits, too!

Families can do so much when they work together. A large storm damaged Tom's neighborhood. All the families help clean up. Everyone in the community helps in some way, no matter what his or her family looks like.

When families get to know each other, they are more likely to **accept** one another. It feels good to be accepted. When everyone is accepted and gets along, we can accomplish so much.

How do you celebrate your family and the families in your community?

HOW CAN YOU HELP?

Is there an elderly couple or family near you? You could offer to help carry in their groceries or walk their dog. You could offer to help with yard work!

GOALS AND TOOLS

GROW WITH GOALS

Accepting all people, no matter what their family is like, is important. Focusing on people's positive qualities will help you be more accepting.

Goal: What makes your family or household unique? What are things that your family or household likes to do together?

Goal: Think of a time you felt empathy toward someone. If you can't think of anything, try to find a time when you can practice empathizing. Do you see someone who looks sad? Ask them how they are feeling and why.

Goal: Get to know someone you haven't spoken with much before. Try to find one thing you have in common or both like.

WRITING REFLECTION

Accepting yourself can help you be more accepting of those around you.

1. What is one thing you like about your family?

2. What is one thing about your family you wish you could improve?

3. What is one thing you can do to be more accepting of others?

GLOSSARY

accept
To agree that something is correct, satisfactory, or enough.

adoption
The action of legally bringing up another's biological child as one's own.

blended
A blended family is one that consists of a couple and their children from previous relationships.

community
A group of people who all have something in common.

divorced
No longer married because the marriage has been legally ended.

empathy
The ability to understand and be sensitive to the thoughts and feelings of others.

foster family
A family that takes a child into its home for a while to care for him or her.

household
All the people who live in a home.

marriage
A legal relationship in which two people are joined as spouses.

related
Belonging to the same family.

support
To give help, comfort, or encouragement to someone or something.

TO LEARN MORE

FACT SURFER

Finding more information is as easy as 1, 2, 3.

1. Go to www.factsurfer.com

2. Enter "**celebratingallfamilies**" into the search box.

3. Choose your cover to see a list of websites.

INDEX

accept 20

adoption 6

arguments 10

blended families 6

celebrate 20

community 5, 6, 19, 20

divorced 6

empathy 15

family members 4, 9, 10, 12

foster family 9

helps 18, 19, 20

household 9

invites 15, 16

learn 16

marriage 6

neighbor 18

neighborhood 19

related 6, 9

respect 12, 15

siblings 12, 13, 15

support 10

understand 15

Blue Owl Books are published by Jump!, 5357 Penn Avenue South, Minneapolis, MN 55419, www.jumplibrary.com

Copyright © 2021 Jump! International copyright reserved in all countries. No part of this book may be reproduced in any form without written permission from the publisher.

Library of Congress Cataloging-in-Publication Data

Names: Colich, Abby, author.
Title: Celebrating all families / by Abby Colich.
Description: Minneapolis: Jump!, Inc., [2021]
Series: Celebrating our communities | Blue Owl Books.
Audience: Ages 7–10. | Audience: Grades 2–3.
Identifiers: LCCN 2019056154 (print)
LCCN 2019056155 (ebook)
ISBN 9781645273684 (hardcover)
ISBN 9781645273691 (paperback)
ISBN 9781645273707 (ebook)
Subjects: LCSH: Families—Juvenile literature.
Classification: LCC HQ744 .C65 2021 (print) | LCC HQ744 (ebook) | DDC 306.85—dc23
LC record available at https://lccn.loc.gov/2019056154
LC ebook record available at https://lccn.loc.gov/2019056155

Editor: Jenna Gleisner
Designer: Michelle Sonnek

Photo Credits: Pollyana Ventura/iStock, cover; Dean Mitchell/iStock, 1; JohnnyGreig/iStock, 3; Africa Studio/Shutterstock, 4; CGN089/Shutterstock, 5; DNF Style/Shutterstock, 6–7; fstop123/iStock, 8–9; triloks/iStock, 10–11; AVAVA/Shutterstock, 12; Don Mason/Getty, 13; FatCamera/iStock, 14–15; kali9/iStock, 16–17; Cultura RM/Alamy, 18; Robert Blouin/Shutterstock, 19; Monkey Business Images/Shutterstock, 20–21.

Printed in the United States of America at Corporate Graphics in North Mankato, Minnesota.